WHAT YOU REFUSE TO REMEMBER

MT Vallarta

Harbor Editions
Small Harbor Publishing

Cover art: "Burning Heart" by Angeli Cabal
Cover design by Allison Blevins
Book layout by Claire Eder

WHAT YOU REFUSE TO REMEMBER
MT VALLARTA
ISBN 978-1-957248-18-9
Harbor Editions,
an imprint of Small Harbor Publishing

For my family:

born from
and chosen

but specifically
Gin Rodriguez
(1996–2022)

Contents

What You Refuse to Remember

"To kill joy . . . is to open a life, to make room for life, to make room for possibility, for chance."

—Sara Ahmed, The Promise of Happiness

I. Recall

Our Song

I was born from a bouquet never received, but stolen. A girl brought home a wilting nosegay of baby's breath and roses. She twirled it in her palm, *dun-dun-dunning* around the house. She twirled buds into the comfort room, whirled them around her hips and thighs while she scrubbed herself pink. She twirled them over her loose sleeping sheet until her legs knotted with fabric and became a pretzel. The next morning, she woke to dried baby's breath and severed rose petals scattered around her scalp. I was in her palms, glowing red, gaping at the dead flowers in her hair. She twirled her handkerchief around me like a tourniquet, cooed: *my crocus, my little digit*. She kissed me. Laughed her language into me. Named me *her only love*.

I dreamt you into fire. We lit vodka in our mouths. One strike and I was ash. The first English words I learned were transmogrified in Tagalog—jingle, rejuice, bomba, bold. *How does this girl only know four words of English, with two for porno?* My mother said I was born in the States but tasted like sugar-apple and cotton-fruit. I ached to taste the flavors up north: *apple peel   pine cone   goose feather   smog.* You grinned, pushed me into a thicket. I learned this is how trees become giants, how flowers bloom so vibrant. The crush of petals on limbs.   Snap of tamarind skins.   The tang of two brown bodies melting.

I finally tasted sky.

My mother said I was born small so I could kiss the ground. Once, I couldn't see for days because dandelion seeds bombarded my eyelids. My mother kissed me and said I still had to go to school. The teacher told me to wash the blight out of my eyes. In the bathroom, a girl tackled me, strangled me with her ponytail. She flushed my body down a well.

Answer this riddle: What leaves but doesn't ache. Blisters but doesn't burn. Scorches with flame, but just pretties into scars.

A g[x]rl doesn't fly. She soars.

Ten Confessions

I remember how easy it was in Los Angeles. How my cardigan always smelled like sun. How I dreamed of being a girl who walks into her grave. How the sidewalk glittered, but ten seconds later, I would step on dog poop or gum. My mother would not let me enter the car.

In our second apartment, I watched a man tie two ropes around two trees. They met in the middle and he fastened a tarp between them. Ten minutes later, his son was in a hammock.

I have lived in three counties: Los Angeles, Alameda, and Riverside. Each one has a problematic relationship with rain. Riverside left my cheeks the most pockmarked. Los Angeles was the hardest to leave.

I once got my little sister to eat a violet. I told her they were the flowers of purple cabbages. I used to imagine I was Laura Ingalls Wilder, not knowing we were little brown monkeys squabbling in the jungle.

My mother taught me how to sob. Like my bones were breaking.

Everyone comments on how well I am healing but I associate well with too fast and I associate fast with ending so I sob alone on Sunday nights and call my best friend and tell him how I wish we were all just books—just paper and spine—so I watch scary movies alone and laugh and laugh as Kiernan Shipka croaks "hail Satan" before being shot.

I clean my toilet, sink, and shower on separate days. I learned how to drive on one-way streets. I have never been in a car accident. I am both my parents' favorite child.

My mother calls me every evening. To make sure I haven't killed myself.

At K-mart, I remember buying discount CDs with my mother. We danced to a scratchy "Night Fever."

I draw plans about jumping into a frozen river. I burn them later.

When You Don't Get Enough R.E.M. Sleep

I have dreams of turning into a broom,
sweeping away the debris we call family.
My mother said I should've been born the eldest,
but instead I am wedged between a shovel and a machete.
My grandfather was a ticket dispatcher at a bus station.
He inhaled smoke until his lungs collapsed.
My grandmother bore eleven children.
One died and she sighed from relief.
After several years, I have finally stopped
biting my nails, but now I am obsessed with
sloughing out the dirt beneath them.
My dentist said I should use an extra soft toothbrush.
I stopped taking edibles and now take
two Buspirone with my tea.
My older sister pitches natural remedies and
somewhere in my chamomile sleep, I chortle.
I pitch a tent under lucky paper stars.
I sleep with a jar of dust, cradling a five-dollar bill
and flyswatter.

The Science of Flowers

I once wrote a report on flowers. I wrote descriptions in my crooked ten-year-old cursive and taped three-week pressed flowers I picked around my neighborhood: *jasmine, dandelion, bougainvillea.* I wrote that jasmines exuded their sweet scents in the evenings; that in some parts of the world, dandelions are used in salads; and that bougainvilleas also grow in the Philippines, particularly up, down, and around the gates of my family's subdivision. I received a B+ for lack of scientific engagement. *I liked reading your stories,* my teacher wrote, *but what about the science?*

According to Kathleen Gutierrez, the Philippines is a site of *imperial botany*: "the movement of botanical knowledge from colonized terrain to Europe . . . to exploit the agricultural potential of [Spain's] overseas empire." When I was younger, my mother said strangers would compare me to a *Japanese flower*. I was a chinky white bud, pale from lack of sun exposure. There is a photo of my family amongst cherry blossoms in Pennsylvania. My mother sent a print back to the Philippines where all my relatives ohhhed and nodded. *Look at them, they pointed, such pale flowers.*

My mother hates receiving flowers as presents. *It's a waste of money. They die in a few days.* My sisters and I chalk it up to her immigrant sensibilities, the survival tactics that taught her anything unsalvageable was wasteful. Our kitchen cabinets are stacked with jam jars and margarine containers. She gets angry when we use more than two squares of toilet paper, furious when we forget to put water in the depleting shampoo bottles. She says flowers in the home are a sign of excess. *Who am I, Doña Victorina?* She screeched when she opened her five-pound English dictionary and saw pieces of bond paper scattered with the faces of squashed and dried flowers. *Who did this?* she asked. *What is this?*

I told her they were the flowers for my project. Her eyes softened. *Won't it be easier if you draw them?* I wished I told her that pressing flowers was proof that they could last. That something as tangible and inevitable as death could be crushed, delayed, and turned into something else. I wanted to write a handbook on pressed flowers, decorate bookmarks, birthday cards, and posters with their eternal colors. Instead, I nodded, *I'll throw them away after.*

One Valentine's Day, my father gifted my mother a balloon and a potted plant. He knew my mother's policy on flowers and thought a plant would be a good alternative. I learned gift-giving was also a science. *Hypothesis: a plant would be a great gift for the mother of my children. Materials: a $5 potted specimen from CVS. Data: wife beyond disappointed. Conclusion: just don't bother again.*

Fifteen years later, I show my parents my new portrait, taken by my partner. The portrait will go up on my new university's website. My parents marvel at the lighting, the bougainvilleas in the background. My mother said we should take more photos outside.

Later, my father drives me home. We pass by the gate where my partner took my picture. I pointed out the contrast of the black iron and violet flowers. "Isn't it beautiful?"

My father nods. "Beautiful," he says, "but what a waste."

I never asked what was wasteful. Beauty, the flowers, or how quickly both expire.

Sesa

At age three, I named myself after a seed.

In Noli Me Tangere, *Sisa is the madwoman. She wanders around San Diego calling and wailing for her lost sons. Later, she sings and dances to the crack of a whip. She dies in the arms of her eldest.*

My mother named me after a saint. Years later, I found out this saint was a colonialist.

In "Remembering Sisa," Ingming Aberia talks about a real-life Sisa. A Sisa he found "moving from place to place . . . searching for her lost sons." He calls her madwoman, even after asking, "What happened?"

At age seven, my appendicitis burst. My father said this can happen when you swallow too many seeds. I worried a watermelon was growing in my belly. Before the operation, my mother whispered prayers like dying sparrows.

Sisa was afraid. She picked up a rock and let it fly.

I mail a rock to my sister. I also sent her an acorn from a cemetery. I asked if she could smell the rain, caress the smoothness of graves.

Sisa was thrown out of the barracks

mostly incoherent   *she said yes to everything.*

The world begins and ends with a madwoman.

Martial Law Trauma

As a child, my mother never let me leave the house.

"For years, activists lived in fear of arrest, detention, and torture
by government agents."

> They moved their families in the dead of night
> one safe home to another
> to evade arrest.

My uncle used to check if his daughter's lips
were still tight.

He would spread her
like a peanut butter and jelly sandwich.

> *Yes,* he said with his finger knife,
> *you are still all right.*

"To this day, we can't find the bones
of all the people he killed."

> A curfew was imposed between midnight
> and four a.m.

I kiss my boyfriend under a falling awning
and my mother grabs me by the ear.

"To this day, it is a struggle to unearth."

        the men took turns interrogating her

        there were different voices

        she could no longer count

        how many different times this happened.

I bang on the walls of my room.

To this day, my mother believes it is a privilege
to stay home.

A Gesture Towards

I am folding myself into an airplane seat. Business class, group A. Surrounded by gray pompadours, pant suits, and briefcases staring at this tiny human in faded leggings and a jean jacket. I want to melt, meld, be stitched onto the surface—any surface—would suffice. It is the middle of October. Los Angeles remains sunkissed and colored. I wonder if I will finally see my father cry. I have one hour—

My sister didn't exhibit the same signs, but they were still there—baggy clothes, hiding behind curtains of hair, going to sleep with her head hurting, waking disappointed that she did not have a tumor. She got a lot farther—water, hands to the neck—while I only dabbled in pills. My mom blames me. Says she must've copied me, but I knew she didn't—her moves were too deliberate. I was too focused on suffering. She wanted to stop everything.

Four years later, I am high on Zoloft. The vomit is a sac of baby spiders hatching from my throat. Seminar hours are closing walls, aching to crush my shoulders. Angry red dots occupy my scalp.

"Your father has a history of mental disorder."

Yes, I know about his brother.

"It's not good to always be in therapy."

"You shouldn't go if you don't want to."

According to Jack Halberstam, queerness is the art of failure. While holding my sister after a month, I thought we must've looked like two kindergarten paintings, two flimsy canvasses swimming with strokes from the clumsiest fingers. I once wrote on a fellowship application that I write poetry because it is the only way I can scream. I didn't get the fellowship.

My mother asks my sister's therapist about *nature v. nurture*. She finally has a theory as to why we are both so fucked. Immigrating to New Jersey left her uprooted, abused, and neglected. In that tiny apartment in East Orange, where my grandmother made snide comments and my father turned a blind eye, her pain made its way through the umbilical cord—to me and then, one and a half years later, to my younger sister. I had to laugh. *Am I a living body of diasporic suffering*. My mother is giving new epistemology to illness.

The Filipino diaspora is a transpacific current of chronic sickness.

Can queerness only be inhabited as pain takes shape. In "Otherwise, Ferguson," Ashon Crawley argues for *otherwise possibilities*: "the disbelief in what is current and a movement towards, and an affirmation of, imagining other modes of social organization, other ways for us to be with each other." When we think of queerness, will there always be a body dangling over an edge. What are other ways we can bend and stretch our limbs, other ways we can mark the gold and brown mapping our skin, other ways we can envelop the adulation and desire clustered in our lips. I look at my bleeding, peeling, stubby fingernails. I tell my father it is okay to cry. I understand why he never told us about my uncle. I understand why he prefers silence; some things can only be communicated in pauses.

I wonder what my father will say when I tell him I am as much his son as I am his daughter.

I have folded myself in pieces. My partner and I name them—yellow, green, orange, and red. Red, I am ready for oblivion. Orange, I am dancing with slivers of light echoing from a blade. Green, a breakdown in the making. Yellow, I can—I think—be happy.

"Your eyes must do some raining if you're ever gonna grow." I wonder what Conor Oberst would say if he sees what I've done to rainbows.

I almost lost my sister to University of California neoliberalism. I like to think my father lost his brother to U.S. empire.

"[T]he violent histories of empire and capital are written on the bodies of Filipinas, on our bruised and bleeding hands and our brown neocolonial breasts."

[Is]   there   [is]   such   a   thing   as

chronic   empire   and   [how]   was   [is]

it   written   [transmitted]

in   [on]   me   [my]
mother].

Kimberly says it's okay to write poems out of marginal notes—a "constellation of hyper-particulars." I am not a constellation—I am a mass of creases, of upset color, of a mind-body waiting, flailing, and beeping for the day when I can wake to possibility. I learned that my uncle also folded himself into a rope. My father found him. I think that was when his mind-body circuits disintegrated and he became machine-operator-paper-boy-company in the morning, busboy-restaurant-worker-best-rice-maker in the evening, and quiet-sleepy-silent-not-really-there-but-not-actually-deadbeat father. What does it mean to be both daughter and familial-emotional-laborer, to be g[x]rl and ghost-of-suicides-past, to be queer death and futurity wrapped in the same potentialities.

"an unrest in [   ] a discontent with [   ] a seeking to conceive [   ]
to wake laughing with tears of joy in our eyes
dreams of [   ] that have us saying:"

I can finally think-feel-bleep-feel I'm alive.

II. Redux

In Which I Become CARDCAPTOR MARIA

I want to be strong like Sakura,
banish my demons into cards,
turn my fears into friends I twirl with.
Sakura wears pink and sometimes her skirts are really short,
but no one seems to call her shameful
or asks her to wear something longer.
I write my new name, CARDCAPTOR MARIA.
My sister says it doesn't match. Sakura is Japanese,
and my first name is too common to be magical.
I pretend the voices in my head are premonitions.
One day, a lady in shadows will give me powers
as I jump across a 300-story skyscraper to greet her.
I get lost in these visions, almost forget my name
is synonymous with laughter. That in my own
fourth grade classroom, no one wants to sit next
to the girl who uses a handkerchief instead of Kleenex.
During recess, I search for loose beads on the playground.
A playground aide asks what I am doing.
I tell her loose beads from broken bracelets
are actually sparkles of magic, and as CARDCAPTOR,
it is my duty to gather them.
She tells me to play with the other children.
I have exhausted the other children.
None of them know what a CARDCAPTOR is,
to the point where they made fun of my sketches
and pointed out again that MARIA doesn't flow well.

I ask my mother why she named me MARIA.
She says it is customary for daughters in the Philippines
to have their first names ascribed to the Virgin Mary.
But we are not in the Philippines, and I don't even know
what a Virgin is! The word is not in my kids' Scholastic dictionary.
CARDCAPTOR is not there either, which means it doesn't exist.
The teacher calls my parents, tells them I spend too much time
daydreaming. One girl laughed at my self-portrait
of stars, frills, and a magic wand like
an ostrich. I throw away my sketches.
CARDCAPTOR SAKURA disappears from Kids WB.
I ignore the voices telling me I am special,
that one day I will find a magic book and a friend,
that my name will belong to something greater
than what I've been given.

Why I Always Hated Juju

Juju taught me the meaning of suicide. It's when you kill yourself first before your mother can kill *you*. She shows me the scar on her neck. During a fight, her mother had silenced Juju by brandishing a knife in her direction. Little did she know that Juju already had a razor blade in her pocket. In one slash, Juju sliced a red line on her neck. It looked like a choker missing its other half. Her mother dropped the knife, locked herself in her bedroom, and cried. Juju went back to the computer and messaged me on AIM.

The other students don't like Juju. They say she talks too much. Some say she's too perky. Some say her happiness is fake because she goes to school in black long sleeves and hoodies even during hot days. Her hair is a curtain slung around her neck. Only I see her scars. One night, I try cutting my own red lines. One prick, and my skin sings.

My parents want to take me to a therapist. Juju shows me a picture of a girl she wants to be—blood-red hair, snow-white skin, and dark lips. She teaches me more words I haven't heard of: Khmer. Mortician. She speaks both languages well. Her brother bought her an electric guitar for her birthday to make her forget a note she found her mother writing. In a script she could not read, her mother wept: *oh dear, oh dear, oh dear, dear me.* Juju blackens my eyes and lips. We go to school, sleeves down. She writes "RIP xxx" on my wrist.

There is a beehive at our hangout. All students are instructed to vacate the quad. Juju is pushed into a rose bush, and I accidentally trample on a ladybug. The first time she came over, she said, "Wow, your house smells just like mine." Lingering stink of fried fish and musk of a sad woman. A guidance counselor takes Juju to the loaner's office so she can change her uniform and accidentally sees a grid criss-crossing up and down her legs. They call her parents.

Juju is upset because a boy she likes likes me. She takes my photo and burns my face over a candle. I learn a boy's lap isn't that soft under your head. A rumor erupts that I like girls and have kissed my cousin. During lunch, I come up to her and say, "I'm glad your mother wants you dead." The other girls cheer behind me and take me under their wing. I hear she went to cry alone by the auditorium, in the spot where shadows make a tent over your head.

Two years later, I am a sophomore in high school. I am wearing my baby blue polar bear pajamas and bopping to pop punk in my ears. My mother hands me the phone. "It's your old friend, Juju." I turn red. I tell my mother to say I'm in the shower.

Gender is a Spectrum, But

Male and female, masculine and feminine, cannot be parsed as some kind of continuum. Rather, sex and gender are best conceptualized as points in a multidimensional space.
—Anne Fausto-Sterling, "The Five Sexes, Revisited"

Somewhere in the early 1990s

I am taking a bath. Water is running from a well. I am with my cousin who has an extra appendage between his legs. I stand like a pair of open scissors and try to relieve myself the way I see him do. My mom swats my hand, telling me that girls sit—or squat—if there is no other way to do it. Next to us, the dirty kitchen smells like fried fish.

A dirty kitchen is a common room in Philippine households. It is so the odors of cooking and preparing food remain separate from the main house.

Somewhere in hetero-futurity 2050

What else do I wear except a white dress. I spent $25,000 in savings. In my arms is the bunny my fiancé and I adopted. His name is Earl and yes, I want children. 3 like my mother, though I worry at least 1 will die, like my father with his brother. I used to care about blood diamonds, but I think the ones on my train were made from cremated dead children from the South Pacific. And if you thought I couldn't leave the house without wearing make-up, you should try going to bed with Korean sleeping packs. There's nothing wrong with wearing a mask, as long as you can still take a breath.

A sleeping pack is a mask Korean women wear to bed. It helps keep your face hydrated the next morning.

Present day

Gender is performative, as Judith Butler says. Gender is
technology, as Jack Halberstam, reiterated by Jenny Sundén,
also say. My brain hurts when I think of x and y axes. I try
to pinpoint the moment—the line, the coordinate—when
my body crossed dimensions, but all I see are ashes from
revelations that once scorched the night. If I could talk
to myself in fours or fives, at what point do my fingertips
stop to feel the same. If a woman's body is a biological time
bomb, what is mine but a wormhole into blinding light.
People think darkness is oblivion, but forget lightning can
also strike.

Emo kid in the early 2000s

I cut my wrists and blacked my eyes into *I'm not okay I promises*. I scribbled *wish I could forget you* on my ex-boyfriend's Converse while the first girl I ever kissed fell into *I let gos* and *dear Maria, count me ins*. Sometimes when I see my students, it's like looking into a mirror where the past never left. My best friend in sixth grade used to gel my baby bangs down everyday, line my lips with the brownest pencil, and taper my flare pants with her extra rubber bands. That was before I switched tracks, when I proved myself with meticulous graphite bubbles even though my mother demanded I be gifted from the start. We lost many kids then. AJ the heroin addict. Rafa with the BB gun. And there was Lexy, who died of cancer before her quinceñera. Sometimes I try to ask Sam if she is where all my memories ended up.

Emo was a movement, a genre, a fashion. Emo was when teen girls got turned on by pictures of boys kissing, and boys could finally be considered attractive when they cried. I used to dream of being one of those boys who would grab another behind his back and kiss while a mosh pit raged behind us. Do I still dream about this? No, not with Gerard Way in retirement.

When was the first time. Was it when I puffed out my chest and tried to imagine hard pecs. When I cried because it hurt to breathe because of this little lump forming, and I cried and I cried to my mother, and she said it was all just normal, normal, normal. Was it when I had no swimsuit but wanted to dive at my cousin's house, so I jumped in the pool with my pink t-shirt in my dad's hands but the boys automatically knew I was not one of them. When did I start wearing lipstick. Was it when I bought that purple shade in college because it reminded me of the plums that once grew in our neighbor's garden. My sister threw up in their living room once because with 3 kids and a father who was always in the warehouse or restaurant, my mom would leave her with the nice ladies who smiled at us during mass. Sometimes, I don't trust myself. There are too many things to mis-remember. If gender is a series of performative acts, what is my memory but a failure in texture.

Whenever you feel yourself start to split, pay attention to the smell of dead cow on this leather chair. How hard is it. How soft. How smooth does it feel.

When do you know you want to be a boy and when do you know you want to be a girl. "Whenever I feel like it" is not a satisfying answer. If I say it depends on the clothes I want to wear, will you be happy. Sam doesn't like dark colors, so she gets upset whenever she rifles through my closet. I like flowers, but I also like skulls, dead people, and pale white boys bleeding from their sockets. Sometimes I worry that the moments I feel the most dude are when I want my fist to lock with another boy's cheek. **Tomorrow** You will get stronger. **Yesterday** You lost your pants in P.E. and cried *I will tremble a prayer. I will beg for forgiveness* in the back of your dad's van. **Next week** You will be lost in a belt of dirty laundry your sister brought home from college. **In the next century** When someone asks how it was growing up in Los Angeles, you will say it was always a fight for space, space, space. *Tired at 20 years old, memory collecting before its time.* What dimension are you from. Is it **A, N, D** like Janelle Monae or **M, F, I** like the rest of society. We cannot answer.

Let me tell you
the girl I kissed
we heard together
my boyfriend tried
my classmates laughed
because I told them my fantasy
a vampire
I just wanted someone to desire
in halves
sometimes I wonder
but the eyes in the mirror
what does it take to meet
if I could exist like this
there truly is an alternate universe

about the time
"hello shitty" was the first song
after school
to pound his fingers into me
during truth or dare
of being turned into
I didn't want to suck blood
a person who always existed
is that really too much to ask
"what really happened to you?"
never answer
the person you were
does this mean inside our brains

It's okay to cry. Just make sure to call me.

I cry. *I'll be just be fine, pretending I'm not.* I'm far from
lonely, but if I rattle hard enough, I'll find her clinking
inside.

North Luzon Expressway

The girl is a baggage of ash,
a quart-sized Ziploc bag of dead flower petals.
A donkey barks in the captain's seat,
his teeth are made of leaves
from Manila-Acapulco Trade palm.
A bone finger pushes a button
and we clatter into a rain cloud
above Mount Santa Rita. "That's
where the Americans watched us,"
my uncle said. The forest green
melds into guerilla warfare black
as the aircraft's wing-tongue
becomes numb with stop. *I want
to go home. But how do you pick
up ash.* The girl sticks the dead flower
stems in her ears. My uncle falls asleep
to dreams of panopticon clouds.
I pour lambanog into snake holes,
hoping one will crush my bones
like Istak's father in *Po-on* except
*we are not rebels. We are tourists
on a trip through fog.* I don't understand
why we don't think of trees as bodies.
The donkey-captain-tour guide meows,
grinding dead petal trail mix
with his palm teeth from the girl
mourning the rotten flowers in her ears.
He says he has seen it all. All the people

who walk through this jungle—white, brown,
yellow, pink, and red—hoping for some
reptile's throat to swallow and cough them up
into dusty pellets. "It's more fun in the Philippines,"
he says, "when you're just a half-animal, half-corpse
waiting to be masticated."

III. Recover

This Is a Story of Two People Who Chose Love

We met in a moment of apocalypse. A month in my lifetime had ended, while yours was still beginning. We kissed over a bottle of Russian vodka. I read you a terrible poem from my blog. You put four fingers inside me. We kissed until the desert sun peeped through the curtains.

You said you remember the evening when I cried over a stuffed blue penguin. I sobbed in your car, and you said you should have ended it then. *What stopped you?* I learned that a group of crows is called a *murder*. You slip a hand under mine, turning my goosebumps into lines.

It has been a year since your lips dangled fire. We moved into an apartment in the city. We sleep in separate rooms, unspoken truths between us. This was when I began showing symptoms. We tried driving our car one night and you found us in the garage, forcing a key through our throat. We throw ourselves on your chest, crying into the sunshine smell of your shirt.

You never forgot that evening. I have blasted that evening. I confess everything to my therapist. She says people like me do not belong in asylums. *You are too high-functioning*. But don't birds lose their breath when they fly too far into space. I start my medicine, hard candies in my stomach.

I worry I will never stop reaching for you. This week, I wanted to call you *honey*. But my parts held me down and twisted my hair into knots. *Isn't it time to put out your own fires?* You cannot quench a house if yours is burning. Like my sisters, we sleep in one bedroom. A twin and bunk bed in both corners.

I am going to die alone in the snow. I am okay with my shadow.

At the Huntington Gardens

Something monstrous turns
my way but is blanketed by the prettiest lilac down
all gushed in purple-white.

—"Mourn You Better," Muriel Leung

Lotus (nelumbo nucifera): once cherished in [   ]; the flower that rises
from the [ ]; continuity; harmony; the belief that your [   ]
won't kill themselves and leave you behind.

I salivate at the thought of your survival.

You wear your cowboy hat and heart-shaped glasses. You send me a picture from the toilet. You already look like a ghost, all burnt and blacked. Like the specter who lives in my auntie's house in the province, only showing herself when there are inhabitants.

A name is a gift. Yours, bestowed by a king.

I laugh at the thought of our families interconnected. Your grandfather, a diplomat to the Philippines; mine, a ticket dispatcher at a bus terminal. We take pictures of phallic cacti, and I sense their needles birthing into us.

Is there silver that could twine us even closer.

Golden barrel cactus (echinocactus grusonii): the largest is more than 85 years old.

I thought you would live to see 30. I wanted to witness this existential crisis. I wanted to see you with your tits out, lips plump, ready to shovel dirt into your grave. I was ready to carve myself onto your tombstone; my finger; your red tomato knife from Costco.

how to stop saying sorry:

1) sew a hook and eye into your mouth

2) regale yourself with the story of the girl from uc [   ]
who was stabbed to death in the student organization offices. blue
pixies glow, spreading their dust around campus. if uc [   ] still
has a building named after d[   ] b[   ], the same man who f[   ]ed
g[   ]'s country, then maybe don't apologize for caring.

3) *makahiya*:   the one that literally   clasps shut

Corpse flower (amorphophallus titanum): it is made of several different compounds

stinky cheese   boiled
cabbage   garlic
rotting fish   sweaty
socks   alcohol dex-
tromethorphan   sodium
nitrate

If you think about death as much as I do
how long until the stench
becomes solid

I want to call your father
I am so sorry   I loved []   I loved [] so much
I want to say I named you "sunflower"

Like him your
light gushes
into petals

Second Person Plural

It's been a week since he ended things. You lie in bed with two fluffy blankets around you. The other parts inside you are asleep. You are the latest sleeper and usually S is the early riser but this time you wake up at 5:00 A.M. and you know why—the text, no, the Instagram message—is burning a bullet hole through your phone. What the fuck was he thinking? What were *you* thinking?

You call your brother, but he doesn't answer. You settle with curling around your blankets like a snake. Foolishly, you start to recall how he held you. His sweaty body was always cold.

You go to the bathroom and wash your face with the frothy face wash. The vanilla bean smell wakes up S. She greets you and notices your puffy eyes. She tastes the salt on your lips.

Later, you huddle together in your shared bedroom. C has built a fire in the middle. You recognize the warmth you always craved as a child. He reminds you that although you were hurt, you were not so innocent either. "You always called him when your world ended." You lie down, your body sinking into the truth.

It feels like there is sand in your mouth. You can't seem to spit out the microscopic granules no matter how hard you heave your throat. Is this what it's like to grieve; if only you could've anticipated this entire year of losses.

A's mother has still not called about a memorial or service.

Four months later, you tell another cis man that you are a survivor. He looks at you with watery eyes, swallows a sip of his drink before saying, "I'm sorry, I'm sorry." He clasps his hands and closes his eyes, whispers his apologies like a prayer. S and C have no idea what he's sorry about.

A month before, your uterus bled for weeks. You stumble your way to the bathroom, lean against the wall. As the toilet fills with red, you imagine the two of you fucking. So far, he is the only one who has satiated your every desire.

"I keep thinking about putting your breast in my mouth." Furiously, he licks your nipple. You feel an everlasting tremor. Later, you are on your stomach as he pushes into you, reminding you that you deserve this fullness, this abundance.

He fed you with his hands and now you wait in the dark, your mouth open.

You are laughing at a joke only you find funny.

You wonder if the people around you think you are crazy. The last time you did this, you were just a child. S and C were in your brain, playing a silly game. Together, you twirled in a circle holding hands until you fell, laughing and gasping for breath. Ten seconds later, you notice the other children in the playground backing away. You want to scream, "You can't catch being crazy!"

On your walk back from the dispensary, you find a burnt mattress on the sidewalk. There are ashes sitting in tiny piles, as if they were spices on sale at the farmer's market. You resist the urge to touch, to anoint yourself.

You wonder if he would've taken a picture of this mattress and ash. He is still following you on IG, watching your stories, liking your posts, sharing pictures of inconsequential things. You wonder if he misses you as much as you miss him. You are so tired of being loved but still feeling empty. You read short stories and watch romantic comedies to satiate your desire for a dream wrapped in a single person. Ever since you learned your parents hated each other, you vowed you would not make the same mistake.

He said he ended things because he knew he couldn't be that person. You go through your assemblage of exes. You conclude the only one who truly loved you was V. He bought you all the presents you wanted. He was with you until the end, until you broke up with him. You never had a love like that since.

You find out he is married and on a Caribbean cruise.

You hear a woman crying. Maybe you've read too many Anne Rice novels. But her sobs are there, echoing in your ears. You know it's not your mother. When she cries, her sobs sound like screams. When she cries, her sobs are screams like rustling orange leaves, dead as they fall to the ground.

There are ghosts in the gardens. As you stand at an alcove watching the drip, drip, drip of a waterfall, you remember your last visit with A. Together, you sat on a bench in the middle of the desert garden talking about endings. You wanted to laugh: *we began in the high desert, but now we're ending in its imitation.* You find an empty table at the center of the path. They recite:

Let us go then, you and I,
When the evening is spread out against the sky
Like a patient etherized upon a table

You lay on the table. CR takes you. As you wrap yourself around him, you see watchful apparitions behind the waterfall, dripping.

She was crying because her notebook was stolen. Straight from her desk. It had the Pochacco stickers all over it. The teacher searches the children's backpacks. Nothing. She cries into her forearms. Her mother barges into the room, demanding what happened. The next day she returns. The teacher acts like nothing happened.

You learn that it's okay to love, but it should never be a reason to stay.

Twelve years later, there are tattoos on your forearms. You still haven't learned how to wink. Somewhere deep in your folds are their houses. You hold hands and twirl in their front yards, spinning.

A letter is sent to A's mother. There is a woman out there, breathing with their lungs.

She becomes a girl trapped in a VCD. She is shimmering in 352x240 pixels. She is sold in Cabanatuan, in a shack next to the wet market.

You have dreams they aren't gone. *I'm not dead.* It breaks your heart to admit that even if they were alive, you would never come back.

How to Continue

find yourself a man who can sleep
with his head on your chest.
hold his hand without asking.
take pictures of ducks fighting in a pond.
drink molotov cocktails on a sidewalk.
text his mother and say you were there
when he waltzed along the blade of a knife.
the night she swam in the salton sea
he proposed to you on a gurney.
how did you answer so affirmatively.
even the ducks in the pond wait ten seconds
before gobbling crumbs. you pick up his hair
and weave it. clasp a collar around your neck.
sometimes it is just difficult to breathe.
hold his hand, feel it grow azure with promise.

In Memoriam

September 30, 2021

Four months ago, my partner and I broke up.

We were together for six years. We met during our first year in graduate school. We clung to each other like lost children. We had sex the first time we kissed. Twenty-four hours later, they told me I was the one. I was the one for years. The one who got lost in a department store in New Jersey. The one who was bullied for being Asian. The one with the traumatic memories. The one who almost made their mother faint with their difficultness.

I shared all these sentences. They strung them around their neck like pearls. We made sangria and slept together locked in my twin bed.

Two months ago, my partner killed themselves.

*Ex-partner. It still takes some getting used to. I blamed myself. I left the sodium nitrate in the file cabinet they inherited. Before we parted, they were so confident. They also found someone else. Another "the one." Someone who could be a better "one" than me.

Their mother texted me the morning she found out they were not going to make it. After visiting them in the hospital, I tried to drown myself in the bathtub. My mother fisted me up to the surface by my hair. Like a newborn fish, I gulped and sputtered.

Two years ago, my partner cheated on me.

Twice. Thrice if I count the time before their death. They kissed two friends and hit on a random girl in a bar. That night, I picked myself apart in the mirror. I plucked strands from my scalp like I did in sixth grade. My mother found bald spots while she slid in barrettes. I refused to go to therapy then. I wish my parents hadn't listened.

Three years ago, my partner proposed to me.

I was crying at their side.
I wish a voice in my head had said,
this is what a trauma bond looks like.
They laid down on their gurney
and wrapped me in an invisible ring.
I have lived in that ring since.

Four months later, my partner is a memory.

They are the neverending dust on photo albums.
The dandelion seed sprouting from the cracks.
The bees that go on, laboring
    in honey.

I have broken
    the invisible
    ring.

I will take
    my time
    becoming
    a memory.

After Anzaldúa

what does love mean at this time
as we dance in the face of our fears but still constantly scorch ourselves
    white.
will I have to yank the septum off your nose while you clamp the
straight-passing onto mine.
will we love in vice grips until we writhe.

how do you speak your second language without feeling yourself
split, a splatter of Manila mango on asphalt.
never getting used to the way smog curls,
tightening itself, singeing our leg hair.
what does the body do when it dies but your bones still squeak
ma'amsir, Hershey, I'll paste it above your pocket.
Ninoy Aquino wants his airport back, thirds never register on the
    x-ray, the petition, the map.

indecipherably, nose bridges pecking, same-same hands brushing nail,
    tip, the first line of fate as we
realize the truth about friction: rubbing, resistance, a surge of
    possibility between two perplexed
bodies.

Notes

The following works were cited in their order of reference:

- Kathleen Gutierrez, *The Region of Imperial Strategy: Regino Garcia, Sebastian Vidal, Mary Clemens, and the Consolidation of International Botany in the Philippines, 1858-1936* (2020)
- Jose Rizal, *Noli Me Tangere* (1887)
- Ingming Aberia, "Remembering Sisa," *Manila Times* (2019)
- Portia L. Reyes, "Claiming History: Memoirs of the Struggle against Ferdinand Marcos's Martial Law Regime in the Philippines," *Sojourn* (2018)
- Robyn Abell Lim, "The proclamation of martial law in the Philippines," *Australian Outlook* (1973)
- Gloria E. Melencio, "Stories of the nameless: eyewitness accounts of Martial Law victims and survivors," *University of the Philippines Los Baños* (2019)
- Jack Halberstam, *The Queer Art of Failure* (2011)
- Ashon Crawley, "Otherwise, Ferguson," *Interfictions Online* (2014)
- Bright Eyes, "Bowl of Oranges" (2002)
- Nerissa Balce, "The Filipina's Breast: Savagery, Docility, and the Erotics of the American Empire," *Social Text* (2006)
- Kimberly Alidio, "Poetic attentions," "The Feeling Archive: Exercises in Queer Asian/American Docu-Poetics," Association for Asian American Studies (2018)
- Judith Butler, *Gender Trouble* (1990)
- Jack Halberstam, "Automating Gender: Postmodern Feminism in the Age of the Intelligent Machine," *Feminist Studies* (1991)

- Jenny Sundén, "On trans-, glitch, and gender as machinery of failure," *First Monday* (2015)
- Hawthorne Heights, "Ohio is For Lovers," *The Silence in Black and White* (2004)
- My Chemical Romance, "I'm Not Okay (I Promise)," *Three Cheers For Sweet Revenge* (2004)
- Silverstein, "Wish I Could Forget You," *When Broken is Easily Fixed* (2003)
- Eighteen Visions, "I Let Go," *Obsession* (2004)
- All Time Low, "Dear Maria, Count Me In," *So Wrong, It's Right* (2007)
- AFI, "Silver and Cold," *Sing the Sorrow* (2003)
- Tsunami Bomb, "20 Going On…," *The Ultimate Escape* (2002)
- Bayside, "hello shitty," *Bayside* (2005)
- The Used, "All That I Got," *In Love and Death* (2004)
- Sara Schat, "For the Love of Lotus," *The Huntington* (2021)
- "Desert Garden," *The Huntington* (Accessed 2021)
- "Corpse Flower (Amorphophallus titanum)," *The Huntington* (Accessed 2021)
- T.S. Eliot, "The Love Song of J. Alfred Prufrock" (1915)
- Gloria Anzaldúa, *Light in the Dark/Luz en lo Oscuro: Rewriting Identity, Spirituality, Reality* (2015)

"Why I Always Hated Juju," "A Gesture Toward," "The Science of Flowers," and "After Anzaldúa" were published in the microchapbook, *The Science of Flowers* (Blanket Sea Press, 2021).

"A Gesture Toward" was previously published in *Nat. Brut*'s "Beyond Resilience" folio (2018).

"In Memoriam" was previously published in *Madwomen in the Attic* (2022).

Acknowledgments

I am blossoming in thank-yous.

To you, dear reader: thank you for taking the time to read this book and hold these words tenderly in your hands. This book would not have been possible without your interest and care.

Thank you to Joan Kwon Glass for choosing this book for the 2022 Small Harbor Publishing Laureate Prize. I am honored you found sweetness and strength in these poems. Many thanks to Allison Blevins and the Harbor Editions team for taking such great care of this book's production. Maraming salamat to Angeli Cabal for the cover art and her incredibly witty illustrations.

This book would also not have been possible without Alana Saltz and the Blanket Sea team. Thank you for giving some of these poems a first home and for believing in *The Science of Flowers*.

One million rose petals to Kundíman: honored to have attended retreat in 2019 (Meg Ryan Forever!) and 2022 (Group #1!). People say Kundíman is a magical place; I have no idea what kind of witchcraft we perform, but there is definitely love, glitter, and sparkles.

To my best friends in every universe: Raymond Sapida, Marie Artap, Aian Mendoza, Muriel Leung, Kazumi Chin, Emi Sawada, Stef Torralba, Lydia Brcak, Kirby Marquez, and Grace Ramilo. Thank you for holding me in your hearts. Shout-outs as well to Angela Peñaredondo, Kimberly Alidio, Izzie Villanueva, Rachelle Cruz, Emperatriz Ung, Eileen Ramos, Kara Pernicano, Michelle Lin, Brian Stephens, Marlen Ríos-Hernandez, Cindy Martinez, and Noah Mullinax for always supporting me and my work.

To UVG: Aurora Santiago-Ortiz, Jorell Meléndez-Badillo,

Vanessa Castañeda, Charlie Geyer, Melanie Plasencia, Joe Blanco, Bryan Winston, Audrey Winston, and Ernesto Mercado-Montero. Thank you for making Dartmouth and the Upper Valley feel like home. Thanks to Sunaina Kale, Shaonta' Allen, Allie Martin, Sa Whitley, Carolyn Choi, Jonathan Cortez, and Son Ca Lam for the wine, cookies, and Uno.

To Jorge Ramírez-Lopez: Thank you for learning and growing with me. I look forward to loving you and going on more adventures with you.

My WGSS colleagues at Dartmouth: Mingwei Huang, Sachi Schmidt-Hori, Eng-Beng Lim, Misty De Berry, Tyler Monson, and Bevan Dunbar. I love chatting, laughing, and eating in Baker Hall with you.

To my mentors and advisors at UCR: Stephen Hong Sohn, Jodi Kim, Sarita See, and Dylan Rodriguez. Thank you for encouraging me to pursue poetry and scholarship.

Much love to the OG mentors: Harvey and Bea Dong. Thank you for owning and operating the best bookstore in the world. Eastwind forever xoxo.

Much love to the Ratanapratums: Maggie, Sonny, Amy, and Alex (1993–2021). Thank you for welcoming me into your family.

Maraming salamat sa pamilya ko: mom, dad, Ate, Thelly, and Rumi. I love you with my entire being. Hugs and kisses to the Yap and Juan clans, especially to Mama Au and Mama Issa for being my second moms, and Ate Jelle, Ate Daday, and Nunoy for being my kapatid.

And last but not least, to Gin Rodriguez (1996–2022). I love you even after the sun dies.

MT Vallarta is a poet and Assistant Professor of Ethnic Studies at California Polytechnic State University, San Luis Obispo. A Pushcart Prize nominee, they are the author of the micro chapbook, *The Science of Flowers* (Blanket Sea). They have received awards and fellowships from Kundíman, Roots. Wounds. Words., The Rowan Foundation, and Philippine American Writers and Artists, Inc. Their poetry is published and forthcoming in *The Selkie, Shō, Nat. Brut, Apogee,* and others. They are hard at work on a research monograph titled *Dismantle Me: Queer, Mad, and Anti-Imperialist Filipinx Poetry.* They were raised in Historic Filipinotown, Los Angeles.

www.ingramcontent.com/pod-product-compliance
Lightning Source LLC
Chambersburg PA
CBHW020212090426
42734CB00008B/1035